Jesus, Pope Francis,
and a Protestant Walk into a Bar

Contents

Introduction

So Jesus, the pope, and a Protestant walk into a bar. The bartender asks, "What will it be today?" As the pope reaches for his wallet, Jesus winks at his companions and says to the bartender, "Just three glasses—and keep the pitchers of water coming."

For almost five hundred years, Catholics and Protestants have been standing together on the common ground of Christ Jesus while at the same time often backed into corners, proclaiming that the other is wrong about what exactly it means to be Christ's church. This sometimes-bitter divisiveness must break the sacred heart of Jesus, who, in his high priestly prayer recorded in John 17, pleaded for his followers to be one.

At times these Catholic-Protestant differences have led to bloodshed—and not just on battlefields hundreds of years ago but in our own era. A prime example is "The Troubles," a three-decade-long conflict that claimed the lives of over 3,500 people in Northern Ireland. All too often, Catholic-Protestant disagreements

1

have resulted in deep family schisms and wounds that fester for generations.

Sometimes the disagreements have resulted simply in hurt feelings because of what seemed like unjust accusations of apostasy. An example is the Vatican document *Dominus Iesus*, published in 2000, which declared that Protestant churches and certain other congregations are not "Churches in the proper sense." In response to that unfortunate declaration, some Protestants produced hurtful and equally inhospitable rebuttals. One of the more tempered and cordial responses came from the prominent German theologian Eberhard Jüngel, who wrote that the conclusion in *Dominus Iesus* actually contradicts many of the recommendations and certainly the spirit of Vatican II. Even within our Catholic and Protestant families, there is sufficient disagreement to keep us befuddled about what it means to be the church.

Yet now and then, though rarely until recent years, Protestants and Catholics have come together in good faith to try to understand each other more fully and to affirm our common commitment to the triune God. A good example of this is the "Common Agreement on Mutual Recognition of Baptism" signed in 2013 between leaders of American Catholics and some American Protestant denominations. Such agreements, we hope, mark a long-desired new chapter in our shared life of faith.

Our often-lamentable history, as well as the approaching five-hundredth anniversary in 2017 of the start of the Protestant Reformation, formed part of the backdrop for a series of sermons that the Rev. Dr. Paul T. Rock led in early 2014 at Second Presbyterian Church, the congregation he pastors in Kansas City, Missouri. The series, "Jesus, the Pope, and a Protestant Walk into a Bar," sought to help listeners understand the remarkable and almost immediate popularity of Pope Francis among many Catholics and Protestants, to say nothing of people of other faiths. Francis had been in office less than a year when the sermons were preached.

From the cover of *Time*, as that magazine's person of the year, to the cover of *Rolling Stone*, Francis began to turn heads immediately upon his surprising election—and not only because he was the first Jesuit pope, the first pope from South America, and the first pope to take the name Francis. Rather, his appeal seemed rooted in his genuine humility, his insistence that the church should be a stalwart defender of the poor, and his desire not to focus on the hot-button culture-wars issues that had so often dominated the papacies of his two predecessors.

Given all that, the time was right to explore what Pope Francis means not just to Catholics but to others as well, including Protestants, many of whom have backgrounds in a wide variety of faith traditions, such as Catholicism. So Rock spent time marinating in the new pope's own writings along with information and insights from others about Francis, the church he leads, and his Jesuit religious order. Rock also asked the congregation's associate pastor, Don Fisher, and its minister to youth, Laura Larsen, each to prepare a sermon for the series. Rock's sermons, as well as those by Fisher ("Being There") and Larsen ("#selfie"), form the basis of the seven sessions in this study. You can view all these sermons online at http://www.secondpres.org/pope-francis-series.

The week Rock preached the first sermon, Second Church member and elder Bill Tammeus, a longtime journalist, devoted his biweekly column in the *National Catholic Reporter* (http://bit.ly/LFZ94x) to the ways in which Francis was finding fans among Protestants. Tammeus inserted into that online column a link to the sermon series that Rock was leading. The result was hundreds of hits beyond the normal number on the church's website. Rock began hearing from people in the Kansas City area as well as from around the world, many of them Catholics. Here are a few examples.

> *From Northern Ireland:* Thank you, Paul, and I pray that God continues to promote Christian unity not only by your teaching but by inviting together people who are truly searching for God's Word alive in today's broken world.
>
> *From Newark, New Jersey:* As a social worker, Catholic, New Yorker/Newark NJ-ite, I am pleased to see the spirit of Vatican II return. I appreciate the sermon focus on what we have in common and staying in the mission of Jesus.
>
> *From a Catholic priest:* Thank you, thank you, thank you. I listened to your sermon three times in a row. You touched my heart and soul, confirming many things I have contemplated. God bless you.
>
> *From Birmingham, Alabama:* I have listened to "Jesus, the Pope, and a Protestant Walk into a Bar" three times now. Have forwarded it to my entire Catholic discussion group. Excellent. What brilliant preaching. (You may not know this, but Catholics aren't used to good preaching.)
>
> *From a Catholic priest in Cairo, Egypt:* I just wanted to thank you for the sermons of Second Presbyterian referring to Pope Francis and the Catholic Church. I am of a mixed Protestant-Catholic family and have considered Martin Luther to be my special patron saint. I truly admire your preaching content/style and look forward to

future sermons. You, your other ministers, and your congregation have inspired me and even made me cry.

In addition, a Catholic youth group from a suburban Kansas City church watched the sermon series online together and discussed each one. Later some musicians from that group participated in a Second Church worship service.

All of this led Rock and Tammeus to respond favorably to a suggestion from Westminster John Knox Press that perhaps the sermon series could form the foundation for a book that would help readers explore Catholic-Protestant common ground, a book that would invite not just ecumenical dialogue but also improved interfaith and interpersonal relations.

If the call of the twentieth century to Americans was to get racial harmony right (obviously still a work in progress), the call of this century is to get religious harmony right. The American religious landscape is becoming increasingly diverse, and it includes a growing segment of people who claim no religious or denominational affiliation at all. Indeed, because of Americans' history as a people who cherish religious liberty, the United States has a rare opportunity to become a model for how people of many religious traditions can live together in harmony. One of the goals of this book is to raise up that possibility and to encourage conversation about how to make it happen.

Therefore, beyond reflections on Scripture, Pope Francis, and the Christian faith, we offer discussion questions to spark enlightening conversation. There also are suggestions for possible next steps of engagement for people who want to take seriously the challenge to understand other faith traditions more deeply and to begin engaging in ecumenical and interfaith discussions and action. Our hope is that all of this reading, discussing, and engaging can lead to a more harmonious religious atmosphere in the country as people replace ignorance with knowledge and even wisdom.

Something you won't find in this book is a detailed history of Catholic-Protestant relations. Others have offered that in books by experts in the field. We have recommended several such Christian-history books in the suggested reading section in the back. And because religious harmony depends on understanding not just other types of Christians but people of other faiths as well, we have also included some books for learning about other major world religions.

It's important to understand that the purpose of authentic ecumenical and interfaith dialogue is not to convert others who are participating in the discussion. Rather, the purpose is simply to know and to be known. This requires humility as well as a willingness to ask nonhostile questions and to listen intently. Beyond that, it takes time and patience to enter into this web of interpersonal, ecumenical, and interreligious discussion, recognizing that participants almost certainly will never reach consensus about matters of faith and recognizing as well that each person's own understanding of this or that matter is never the final one. In other words, it is helpful to adopt the fascinating attitude of both tentativeness and assertiveness found in Talmudic culture, where rabbis disagree with each other in a spirit of respect and with a common goal of engaging matters of faith ever more deeply. As a result, we all become better people of faith and better humans.

In some ways, we might do well to let our children lead us in this. They often seem to have a capacity both for curiosity and for making friends with people outside their own families and their own racial, ethnic, and religious groups. Ecumenical and interfaith dialogue also seems to succeed more often when participants do more than sit around a table and talk. Indeed, when people work together on common projects, such as building Habitat for Humanity houses or working in a soup kitchen, they quickly come to recognize that people they had thought of as different and even weird are much like themselves.

Dialogue and other connections between and among people of different faith traditions are not meant to lead to a syncretistic faith that all can hold in mushy common without much disagreement. That's an unworthy and unnecessary goal. Rather, ecumenical and interfaith relations work best when all participants remain true to their own tradition even while being open to understanding the traditions of others. The mandate, in other words, is to be both deep and wide.

We hope this small book will help to guide you toward that theological depth and width so that you are free to be who you are and free to let others be who they are, all the while doing justice, loving mercy, and walking humbly with God.

Chapter One

Unusual Pedigree

The next day Jesus decided to go to Galilee. He found Philip and said to him, "Follow me." Now Philip was from Bethsaida, the city of Andrew and Peter. Philip found Nathanael and said to him, "We have found him about whom Moses in the law and also the prophets wrote, Jesus son of Joseph from Nazareth." Nathaniel said to him, "Can anything good come out of Nazareth?" Philip said to him, "Come and see." When Jesus saw Nathanael coming toward him, he said of him, "Here is truly an Israelite in whom there is no deceit!" Nathanael asked him, "Where did you get to know me?" Jesus answered, "I saw you under the fig tree before Philip called you." Nathanael replied, "Rabbi, you are the Son of God! You are the King of Israel!" Jesus answered, "Do you believe because I told you that I saw you under the fig tree? You will see greater things than these." And he said to him, "Very truly, I tell you, you will see heaven opened and the

angels of God ascending and descending upon
the Son of Man."

John 1:43–51

Catholic versus Protestant. It manifests in a myriad
of ways: Green or orange. Priests or pastors. Mass
centered around the table, or worship services centered
around the pulpit. Transubstantiation, consubstantia-
tion, or just a memorial? Birth control or not so much?
Weekly confession or going straight to God ourselves?
There are so many ways to see so many things differently.

When John Fitzgerald Kennedy became president
in 1961, our national Protestant identity shuddered.
Many Americans believed that in one way or another,
the pope would now be running the United States from
his Vatican office. In those anxious years in the '60s, my
Aunt Katie fell in love with and married a Catholic man
named Carmen Grillo. My aunt's grandfather, my great-
grandfather, was a Presbyterian minister who served
congregations in northern Wisconsin. He was a good
man and devout Christian, but when he learned that his
granddaughter was determined to marry a "papist," he
made it clear to the family that he would be seeing her in
hell. It's a nice little story we like to recount around the
Thanksgiving table. Regretfully, I'm sure many families
can tell similar tales.

We could easily spend our energies and passions
rehashing disagreements and wounds. Catholics and
Protestants each have their share of historical and doctrinal faults that can be used to fuel frustrations and ste-
reotypes. But I think we would all agree that our time
would be better spent celebrating and exploring why it is
that this new pope seems to be bringing us together when
religion so often tears us apart.

It's like he's missed the monumental scope of the thing. Pope Francis just doesn't seem interested in or care much about the fact that he has inherited the throne of St. Peter. He's not impressed with being the supreme pontiff, the Holy Father, the keeper of the keys of heaven. Despite this, or perhaps *because* of his meek approach, Francis has entirely shifted the focus of Catholic leadership from an obsession with ecclesial virtue and doctrinal policing to a joyful tending to the wounded. How has this welcome shift taken place so quickly? The plain answer is this: Pope Francis is walking in the simple, profound, and challenging footsteps of Jesus, the Messiah who grew up not in the gilded halls of ecclesial power but in a trailer park called Nazareth.

Jorge Mario Bergoglio has been making headlines since white smoke floated above the Vatican in April 2013. Much of his immediate impact has to do with where he came from and the perspective through which he views the world and his role as the bishop of Rome.

Pope Francis grew up nowhere near Rome, not to mention Europe. He is a mixed-race Latino born on the dark-skinned side of the equator—the "heathen hemisphere," as it used to be known by Europeans. He is the first pope to receive his training and ordination after the radical reforms instituted by Vatican II (some changes take a few generations to sink in). He is also the first Jesuit pope. Jorge Bergoglio has been gently stirring the waters, winning fans and frustrating advocates of the status quo from day one. And he's doing so not through papal edicts from his Vatican office or moral pronouncements from St. Peter's Basilica but rather by:

- Washing the feet of teen felons on Maundy Thursday rather than the feet of cardinals and bishops, which is customary.

- Selling the papal Harley to raise money for the poor. (Did you realize there was a papal Harley?)
- Forgoing the papal suite and living in a guest room on the Vatican grounds.
- Driving around in a Ford Taurus or taking public transportation, all of which makes millionaire bishops and capitalists around the world quite uncomfortable.

This is a pope who is reminding people that the primary work of the church is to be an instrument of Christ's reconciling grace and love—to be, as he says, a "field hospital on the battleground of life"—and modeling this by touching and embracing those who have known rejection and pain for too long; by inviting homeless men and their pets to his birthday party; by serving Communion to divorced women; by embracing atheist leaders as children of God; by spontaneously picking up hitchhikers in his Popemobile; and by allowing children who wander onto the papal stage while he addresses the crowd to give him a hug and sit on his chair.

All of this is happening through a church leader who is, by his own admission, a sinner, a leader who is bringing us back to the basic principles that unite us. I believe that through this humble pope, Christ is nudging Catholics and Protestants to stop focusing on all that we're against and instead celebrate and advance all that we are for. Such a change in perspective can be achieved by remembering who we are and where we are from. The fact is, the more centralized and established, sedentary, clean, and dominant our faith becomes, the less attractive and engaging it becomes for those who have been dominated, feel unclean, and are marginalized and need to experience God's love the most.

Come and See

"Can anything good come out of Nazareth?" asks Nathanael. You see, Nazareth was a small agricultural town of maybe 1,000 residents in the first century. Fifteen miles to the west were bustling port cities along the Mediterranean. Fifteen miles to the east was the Sea of Galilee and the Jordan River that ran down to Judea and Jerusalem. Nazareth was an in-between place, and these in-between Nazarenes spoke a crude dialect. They were understood, by and large, to be a less cultivated lot. And it was here, in Nazareth, that Jesus the Christ, most likely known by many as Mary's bastard child, spent most of his formative years.

In the first chapter of John's Gospel, Jesus has grown into a young rabbi and is beginning the process of choosing his first disciples, those who will share in his work of revealing and advancing the kingdom of God. It's interesting, and quite telling, to notice what wasn't part of Jesus' interview process. He doesn't begin by asking for a statement of belief. He doesn't ask Philip about his views on Passover or on the perpetual purity of his mother Mary. He doesn't ask for a paper on predestination or apostolic succession. So what does he say? Not much. Just "Follow me." And Philip does. It must be that Jesus came across as someone quite accessible. Someone immediately relatable. Someone followable.

So Philip follows him, and when he tells his friend about this remarkable rabbi, Philip is met with Nathanael's dismissive comment, "Can anything good come out of Nazareth?" Philip responds beautifully. He doesn't begin by unwinding a complex Christology or defending the new rabbi and his pedigree; he simply invites his friend to find out for himself and says, "Come and see!" Follow me. Come and see. Not a lot of explaining or defining, just give it a try. Often it's as simple as that.

One of the many things I like about this new pope is that his first and primary message has been similar, "Come!" If you're divorced, gay, disfigured, a felon, desperately poor, come. You are loved. It's an incredibly powerful and simple message, and yet the more we have formalized and codified our faith and grown comfortable with our denominational processes or structures or authority, the more our words, rituals, formality, and polity communicate to outsiders (even though we don't mean to) that, actually, they are not so welcome. Outsiders never felt this way with Jesus.

After Nathanael meets Jesus and Jesus shares a few of Nathanael's personal details, a befuddled Nathanael, shocked into the realization that he is standing before someone quite remarkable, shakes his head and asks, "How do you know me?" If I were to extrapolate on Jesus' response, he answers, in effect, "I don't just know you, Nathanael. I know where you've been. I know where you come from. I know you think me irrelevant because I'm from Nazareth. But before you consider following me, you need to know that my kingdom begins on the margins and doesn't have much to do with pomp or regal dominance. Leadership in my kingdom is about becoming a conduit of grace, a bridge, a ladder upon which angels ascend and descend; it's about becoming a person through whom heaven can be made accessible to imperfect people and imperfect people can experience a touch of heaven." This will be Jesus' message throughout his ministry: Greatness is not what those at the center of power know it to be. True greatness is God embodied in a Nazarene and what those on the margins are searching for; it's a place of belonging, and it's One with whom and to whom they can belong.

While we tend to focus on power centers like Rome and Jerusalem, God is at work on the frontier, spreading a different sort of power that makes a lot more sense to those who know what life is like in the rough places. The result can be a faith that comforts those who are troubled and often troubles those who are a little too comfortable.

This pope is a Jesuit from Argentina, a nation that has known the upheaval of revolution and coups, Marxist ideology, and military rule. This is a pope who himself was caught up in the struggle between poor, radical priests and the state power that opposed them. As a bishop, he regularly celebrated Mass in the slums of Buenos Aires. This practice of walking and associating with the poor comes from the order of priesthood he chose to follow—namely, the Society of Jesus, otherwise known as the Jesuits. The Jesuit order was founded by Ignatius of Loyola in the 1500s with an emphasis on poverty, mission, community, and discipline.

As Francis described it in an interview for *America* magazine in September 2013, the Jesuit order is not centered on its own preservation or advancement. It is centered on Jesus Christ. Jesuits live in constant tension because they try to live lives that are focused on the margins, on the frontiers, on the horizon, looking for signs of Jesus. This, Jesuits would say, forces them to be creative, searching, and generous. As Francis has put it, "There is always the lurking danger of living in a laboratory. Ours is not a lab faith but a journey faith. . . . You cannot bring home the frontier, but you have to live on the border and be audacious."

The reason the pope has chosen to live in a Vatican guest room rather than the papal apartment is because, in his words, the papal apartment is spacious but has a very small entryway. As a result, it was difficult for people to enter and visit. As a Jesuit, Bergoglio was used to living in community—praying together, welcoming guests, encouraging one another, living life, and doing mission together. "Community for Mission" is one motto of the Jesuit order. Even as bishop of Rome, the pope has chosen to live in a guest room and share life with other priests as he seeks to follow Jesus and invite others—everyone, it seems, into the faith—not to police practices or parse doctrine, but to come and see and follow Jesus.

A Frontier Faith

Another thing that makes Pope Francis so fascinating is the way in which he has captured the imaginations of millions—not only the faithful or those comfortable with the status quo but those on the frontier, of various faiths and life conditions who had given up on the church. Francis has elevated the healing mission of the followers of Jesus—the church as servant and comforter, as bruised, wounded, and dirty because it has been on the streets rather than assembling in cathedrals, concerned about preservation.

As Americans, we might not always feel like it, but we are a powerful people. Ours is the wealthiest nation in the world, and the vast majority of us have all kinds of resources at our disposal. Those of us who can afford it spend much of our time distancing ourselves from the Nazareths, the slums of our cities as well as our own lives, which makes all the sense in the world. Slums, after all, are not comfortable places. They can be unpredictable, governed by different rules and priorities. But we were never called to live a pristine faith, a domesticated faith preserved or perfected in a church building or a laboratory of devotion. It is from the margins that our God walks and calls and speaks to us and says, "I know where you are from. Follow me—but not to a place of comfort, not to a throne room, not to a place of centralized power. That's not where I'm going. Together we will discover and define what this kingdom is all about. Together we'll redefine power and prominence. Come and see."

There are many who have given up on the church—many who feel too rejected, too dirty, too foreign, too uncivilized, too far removed from the rigors of piety, church rules, and expectations. Does anything good come out of Nazareth? Apparently God does. Come. Let's be the kind of people who are committed not to what divides but to what unifies us Protestants and Catholics, Nathanaels and Philips. Let's follow Jesus.

Let's Talk about It

1. Pope Francis attained remarkable worldwide popularity in his first year in office. But popularity can be fleeting. How would you rate his appeal today? What has changed and why?

2. What do you most admire about Pope Francis? What about him and his papacy gives you pause?

3. If a Catholic asked you why you're a Protestant (or vice versa) would you—could you—respond, in effect, "Come and see"? If so, what would they see?

4. If, as Jesus and Pope Francis contend, real power is dirty, simple, smiling, inviting, and on the margins,

is your congregation demonstrating such power to the world? How? If not, what might you do to help create such ministry?

5. In what ways have you or your congregation distanced yourselves from the slums of the world—literally or figuratively—and what can you do to change that? Conversely, in what ways have you or your congregation responded to the needs of the slums and embraced that reality as your own?

Chapter Two

A Different Kind of Leadership

Jesus said to them, "Come and have breakfast." Now none of the disciples dared to ask him, "Who are you?" because they knew it was the Lord. Jesus came and took the bread and gave it to them, and did the same with the fish. This was now the third time that Jesus appeared to the disciples after he was raised from the dead.

When they had finished breakfast, Jesus said to Simon Peter, "Simon son of John, do you love me more than these?" He said to him, "Yes, Lord; you know that I love you." Jesus said to him, "Feed my lambs."

John 21:12–15

Some days I can grow rather cynical about the assortment of leaders in our world. I find myself searching for those larger-than-life personalities that, ideally, provide examples, models, and life-styles that help us bend our communities toward the truth.

And then there are days when I notice the generous supply of amazing, normal leaders I get to rub shoulders with on a regular basis—those who give up hours every month to dream and lead the way in helping the church become the hands and face of Christ to our neighbors. There are so many people who, in various ways, lead in large and simple, silent and selfless ways, day after day, choosing to see and remedy the needs of others over their own. These are people who regularly put their wants aside and serve others, taking on the unglamorous jobs and doing not just what is easy but what is right.

There are many normal and inspiring leaders in our communities. Yet sadly, it seems those who receive a disproportionate amount of the spotlight and attention are people who model the sort of sensational but disappointing leadership that is attention grabbing and arrogant. This is leadership that we know in our guts is wrong both in its impetus and example. From professional athletes who unleash embarrassingly egotistical tirades to brash governors whose stubborn agendas and denial of the truth grow firmer and more wearying, to church leaders who turn a blind eye to abuse, to generals and politicians who draw lines in the sand and stand on morally righteous pedestals while demonizing their rivals.

As everyday leaders and global citizens, we are thirsty for an example of authority that speaks and lives out and models ideals we know are right even if they are hard to hear. This is another reason why the more I read and learn about Pope Francis, the more I appreciate his choices, his style, and the type of leader he has chosen to be.

The kind of leader he has become has a lot to do with how he lives. There are plenty of leaders who determine positions and make their proclamations from a place of privilege or behind impressive desks in ivory towers, but this pope seems to be most comfortable and confident on the streets. The life-style choices he has made are hard to argue with. So too, the truths he speaks—truths I some-times don't want to hear—resonate with our souls. It is clear where this pope draws his inspiration for leadership.

Leadership, Jesus Style

In the twenty-first chapter of the Gospel of John there is a powerful story that has everything to do with leader-ship, even though the word is never mentioned. In subtle yet significant ways, Jesus' life and interaction with his disciples after his resurrection illustrate what great lead-ership looks like.

> After these things Jesus showed himself again to the disciples by the Sea of Tiberias; and he showed himself in this way. Gathered there together were Simon Peter, Thomas called the Twin, Nathanael of Cana in Galilee, the sons of Zebedee, and two others of his disciples. Simon Peter said to them, "I am going fishing." They said to him, "We will go with you." They went out and got into the boat, but that night they caught nothing.
>
> Just after daybreak, Jesus stood on the beach; but the disciples did not know that it was Jesus. Jesus said to them, "Children, you have no fish, have you?" They answered him, "No." He said to them, "Cast the net to the right side of the boat, and you will find some." So they cast it, and now they were not able to haul it in because there were so many fish. That disciple whom Jesus loved said to Peter, "It is the Lord!" When Simon Peter heard that it was the Lord, he put on some clothes, for he was naked, and jumped into the sea. But the other dis-ciples came in the boat, dragging the net full of fish,

for they were not far from the land, only about a hundred yards off.

When they had gone ashore, they saw a charcoal fire there, with fish on it, and bread. Jesus said to them, "Bring some of the fish that you have just caught." So Simon Peter went aboard and hauled the net ashore, full of large fish, a hundred fifty-three of them; and though there were so many, the net was not torn. Jesus said to them, "Come and have breakfast." Now none of the disciples dared to ask him, "Who are you?" because they knew it was the Lord. Jesus came and took the bread and gave it to them, and did the same with the fish. This was now the third time that Jesus appeared to the disciples after he was raised from the dead.

When they had finished breakfast, Jesus said to Simon Peter, "Simon son of John, do you love me more than these?" He said to him, "Yes, Lord; you know that I love you." Jesus said to him, "Feed my lambs." (John 21:1–15)

Do you catch what Jesus the leader did here? What exactly did he do? He showed up. He anticipated and provided for basic needs. He asked good questions.

In this passage from John, the resurrected Jesus came to his disciples on the shore after they had gone back to fishing. Fishing was what they knew. It was their fallback plan. They were fishermen, and, apparently, Peter enjoyed fishing naked, but back to Jesus. This was the third time the resurrected Christ had come to the disciples in John's Gospel and found them doing what was known and comfortable. But on this occasion, doing what they did best, the fishermen were having no success. And so Jesus called out to them from the shore.

If I were Jesus on that morning, I know what I would have called out, because just a few chapters earlier Jesus had made explicit what he was going to do and what he expected his disciples to do. He told them that he would be killed and resurrected and that their job was to go into the world and share the good news of the kingdom of God. So, knowing my impatient self quite well, I would have said something like, "Hey guys! Really? What *are* you doing here? I honestly don't remember saying *any-thing, anything at all* about returning to your boats on the Sea of Galilee. In fact, I clearly said you would be my witnesses to *the world*, not the waves. What's the story?" Thankfully, that's not what Jesus says.

Instead, before he speaks any words and before he shares any truths, he comes to where they are three different times. This time, when he does finally speak, Jesus begins with a question. There's no hint of shame in his words. He doesn't point out the obvious mistakes. He doesn't reprimand them for their lack of obedience. He comes to them and asks a question, and then he asks another. He listens, and finally he shares some helpful advice.

Be Present, Be Humble

It's a different kind of leadership that Christ models here. It's beautiful, it's subtle, and it compels his disciples into relationship, new perspectives, difficult transitions, and new solutions. Most of us tend to approach mistakes or misunderstandings with assumptions or reactions that lead to defensiveness and inertia because our approach is neither vulnerable enough nor bold enough to empower and encourage the change that is needed. Leaders who choose to lead like Jesus have the guts to acknowledge things that are a whole lot easier to ignore and to speak the truth without a residual tone of accusation. They shine a light on the situation in a way that doesn't demean or assume. They speak the truths that we actually, in the corners of our souls, long to hear. "You haven't caught anything, have you?" Jesus asks the disciples. And, similarly, he gently whispers to our hearts, "Are your career decisions in line with the kind of person you want to be?" "Is your relationship getting the attention it requires?" "Are you beginning to lean on that unhelpful habit again?" "Are you treating your daughter, your neighbor, your colleague the way you'd want to be treated?"

How does Christ do it? How does he speak the truth in love without shame? He begins by coming to us. He doesn't pontificate through a bullhorn. He doesn't level pronouncements and point out our driving errors from the backseat. Christlike leaders take the time—once, twice, three times—to be with people right where they are. Before they speak words of instruction, they watch, they ask questions, and they listen. Jesus found his depressed and frustrated disciples not doing what they were supposed to be doing. Rather than react like I would have, he patiently stood and watched, and then finally asked them a question: "Have you caught any fish?"

I like that about this pope. He doesn't seem to preach. When you think about it, preaching isn't typically received very well by anyone. None of us likes to be preached at. When he teaches or shares a challenging word, Francis doesn't sound like he is talking down or scolding (except sometimes to his own aloof cardinals). Instead, he seems more preoccupied by and interested in healing. *Time* magazine's Nancy Gibbs put it this way: "This Pope has not so much changed the words as he has changed the music." Humility is the tone that makes the truth far easier on our ears.

When we know that someone has crossed time and space to be with us right where we are, whether what we are doing is right or wrong, it frees us up to accept truth because it is coming to us from relationship with us, not from a place of righteousness that preaches at us.

As Jesus stands on the shore and speaks to his friends from a place of presence and humility, the disciples finally acknowledge the truth of their fruitlessness. *He's right. We haven't caught one fish all night. We need to do something drastically different.* We've all done it. We've all spent seasons in our boats doing what is familiar: throwing the nets out and gathering them in over and over with the same results, falling back into those old practices even though we know they aren't especially productive. Bringing one season to a close and shifting into the next can feel like an overwhelming and impossible task, but what a gift it is when we have leaders who look like friends. These leaders come to us and walk with us and speak the truth in love, providing the stability and honesty we need to navigate the pains of change.

With his stooped gate, his joyful and humble demeanor, his thick glasses, his affiliation with the poor, and his orthopedic loafers, Pope Francis seems comfortable with people. And he is comfortable for people. Standing with and among, he is able to point out the holes in our society's fishing nets that are causing us to struggle with the same problems across cultures. In his apostolic exhortation in November 2013, he says things like, "Today everything comes under the laws of competition and the survival of the fittest. As a consequence, masses of people find themselves . . . without possibilities, without any means of escape." That sort of prophetic truth hurts because it is painfully accurate.

For many of us "intellectuals" of the faith, Francis gently but firmly challenges our penchant for discussion and debate rather than action and messy involvement in the struggles of the world. As he told *America*, "If the Christian . . . wants everything clear and safe, then he will find nothing. [For] those who long for an exaggerated doctrinal 'security,' who stubbornly try to recover a past that no longer exists . . . faith merely becomes an ideology among other ideologies." That hits close to home, doesn't it?

But what makes such pointed truths palatable coming from this pope is that when he speaks of the poor and things such as the growing disparity of wealth in the world, he does so not from the safe distance of a Vatican tower but—having opted out of the comfort of ecclesial wealth and privilege—from the soup kitchens and the poorest barrios. Leaders who follow the example of Christ don't pontificate—they join. They speak with humility as they stand with those they hope to serve and lead.

As Teddy Roosevelt put it in his famous "Man in the Arena" speech, "It is not the critic who counts, not the man who points out how the strong man stumbles, or where the doers of deeds could have done them better. The credit belongs to the man who is actually in the arena, whose face is marred by dust and sweat." Leaders are those who speak from within the ring, those who incarnate themselves into situations and lives and love the people they seek to lead through pain and into the promise.

What's the Point?

Finally, leaders keep the larger purpose in mind and out front in the midst of the urgent and ever-present minutiae in order that the greater good of God's kingdom is advanced.

It's been said that effective leaders live in the present, appreciate the past, and create the future. That's a tall order, but it's achieved more effectively when the big picture and the end game are kept front and center. We all tend to find comfort and security in those things we know how to do and those things we've done repeatedly, even if we don't do them well. You can imagine the disciples finding comfort amid their grief in the routine of unfolding nets, arranging their gear on the boat, and pushing from the shore. They tell the old stories as they throw the net out over the water, watch it fall, haul it in again, and repeat. Such rituals are reassuring, stabilizing, something on which we can depend.

But wise leaders remember that in the long run, the purpose of going fishing is to catch fish. Leaders remind us not to lose track of our ultimate purpose. "You haven't caught any fish, have you?" Having diagnosed their trouble, Jesus doesn't just encourage the disciples to adjust their net-tossing technique or tell them to let the net settle a little longer. "No," he says, "pull your nets in, shift your focus, and turn in the opposite direction. Cast your nets from the other side of the boat."

Christlike leaders often call for a radically new perspective on a well-worn and oft-repeated task so that the larger and deeper original goal is accomplished. But what exactly are the goals we are working toward in the first place as followers of Christ? What is the larger purpose? After the disciples have filled their nets with fish and made their way to shore, they find Jesus waiting for them, having built a fire and prepared some breakfast. After filling their bellies and warming their bodies, Jesus asks the most important question of all, a question that points us to the largest purpose, the ultimate truth from which our most important work and best selves proceed: "Do you love me?" It's that profoundly simple and that profoundly serious.

Our answer to this question is the basis of everything we do. "Do you love me?" If you love me, Jesus says, then feed my sheep. Go do whatever you feel gifted and called to do as part of the community. Go fish. Go be a social worker, go be a parent, go be a writer, go be a lawyer, go be a community activist, go be a church member. Do what you feel called to do, but always know in your heart why you are doing it. Whatever we do in this world of ours, as children of God, should find its motivation in love. And that love should be rooted and growing in our understanding of God's love for us. If we can't trace what we're doing back to love, then we've lost our way. We're in the wrong boat and are fishing with faulty nets. We've forgotten the larger purpose, the why. And if we're not plugged in to the larger purpose, the why, then it's time to stop and ask some hard questions.

Chris Lowney, a man who studied to become a Jesuit priest and then went on to be a successful investment banker, has recently written a book on Francis. Lowney says that Francis probably would not articulate a particular leadership philosophy according to Harvard Business School standards. Yet in watching how he leads and from where he leads, it is clear that his focus is singular. Francis knows deeply that he is loved by God, and with every word and act he seeks daily to return that love and follow after Jesus Christ. The One who knows us and loves us completely asks, "Do you love me?" Then he tells us to go and feed his sheep.

Let's Talk about It

1. Do you agree that "the leaders who receive a disproportionate percentage of the spotlight and attention on the world's biggest stages are people

who model the sort of sensational leadership that is attention grabbing and overconfident"? Can you think of some examples of this? Do you ever see this in faith communities? Are you ever guilty of this kind of leadership? When you see it or embody it, what's the most redemptive way to respond?

2. What stands out to you about Jesus in this story from John 21? Do you find it difficult to be present with people before instructing or critiquing them, or to acknowledge painful truths with clarity, grace, and humility? Do you see such abilities in Pope Francis? Do you see them in the leaders of your faith community? What do they look like when they are on display?

3. What difficult realities have been called to your attention by Jesus or another leader? What made his or her words so powerful? What difference does it make when a leader speaks not from on high but down "in the arena" with you?

4. If one job of leaders is to keep the big picture in mind at all times, how do they avoid simply being endless dreamers with no conception of why it's also important to pay attention to the necessary details? Or are leaders either dreamers or detail people but rarely both? If so, how should the leadership of religious communities be structured so that both approaches are included?

5. What habits or decisions in your own life might be different when considered through the lens of Jesus' big question: "Do you love me?" How might things be different within and between various religious groups if leaders put love first?

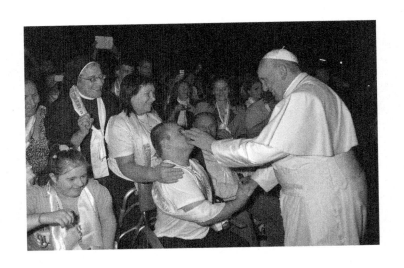

Chapter Three

Being There

"With what shall I come before the LORD,
  and bow myself before God on high?
Shall I come before him with burnt offerings,
  with calves a year old?
Will the LORD be pleased with thousands of rams,
  with ten thousands of rivers of oil?
Shall I give my firstborn for my transgression,
  the fruit of my body for the sin of my soul?"
He has told you, O mortal, what is good;
  and what does the LORD require of you
but to do justice, and to love kindness,
  and to walk humbly with your God?
                                    Micah 6:6-8

In 1882, President Justo Rufino Barrios of Guatemala, looking for ways to lessen the influence of the Catholic Church in social and political life, went to New York City and invited the Presbyterian Mission Board to establish a presence in his country. One John Clark Hill, who was just about to get on a slow boat to China, heard the call and redirected his plans to Guatemala. Barrios provided Hill with land abutting the national plaza in Guatemala City, adjacent to the Catholic cathedral. To this day, Central Presbyterian Church stands one block from the center of the city, and, to my knowledge, Guatemala City is the only capital in Latin America with a Protestant church right in its heart.

In general, the Protestant churches of Guatemala define themselves as anti-Catholic. They use no candles, because Catholics use candles. They use no crosses, because Catholics have many crosses. They serve Communion very infrequently, because Catholics offer the Eucharist every day. They consider Catholics to be non-Christian. They have giant public address systems even in their little tiny worship spaces so as to send the gospel message out into the streets, to be heard by the lost souls passing by.

Where did they learn those kinds of ideas? Where did they get such perspectives? Answer: from the 1950's Protestant churches of North America. That's who we used to be, right? Many of us grew up under that kind of influence.

I grew up under the strong warnings of my grandmother about the dangers of Catholicism. I remember the little book she gave me called *High Is the Wall* about the pitfalls of marrying a Catholic. As it turned out, some of my best friends were Catholics, not to mention some girlfriends. So I was in a conundrum early on.

Thank God we've evolved. While some of our elders and deacons and other faithful church leaders at Second Presbyterian are former Catholics, the backbone of many Catholic churches is comprised of former Presbyterians. We Protestants have discovered that some of our best church music and our best spiritual practices come from Catholics, not to mention the immense contribution of Catholic scholarship to our theological education. The Catholic hymnal has included Martin Luther's "A Mighty Fortress Is Our God" for decades now. The migration goes both ways.

My own experience as a pastor in small towns leads me to say, "Thank God for the Catholics." I usually had more in common theologically with the priest in town than I did with most of the Protestant pastors, who in those settings tended to tack just to the right of Attila the Hun in their biblical understanding and application. I probably learned more from the Catholics—clergy and lay—in weekly Bible study than I did in seminary.

Because of how our Protestant-Catholic relations have evolved, I am confident that Guatemalans will also get there someday. Though our responsibility to them probably includes helping them unlearn much of what they learned from us, they'll probably do it just fine on their own as Catholics and Protestants there discover God's goodness in one another.

Partnership across Differences

A mission group from our church recently went to Guatemala and while there met with several women who had organized a health center for their community under the leadership of Juana Herlinda Yac, a leader in women's ministry in Maya Quiche Presbytery. Of particular interest to me was how these women named their church connections when they introduced themselves. In addition to the Presbyterians, there were women from some Pentecostal churches and at least one Catholic.

In another setting, I was able to ask Herlinda about cooperation with Catholics. Looking around the room at the number of Presbyterian ministers (all male) who were present, she lowered her voice and said, "I can't say too much about it here, but yes, women from all kinds of churches work together on our community health issues. We do just fine. We're all in the kingdom of God working together."

That's how it happens. Common concerns—God's concerns, gospel concerns—break down old religious barriers.

That's what's so exciting about Pope Francis. It seems that new life is being breathed into Micah's ancient encouragement—what is sometimes called the height of Old Testament theology: "To do justice, and to love kindness, and to walk humbly with your God" (Micah 6:8). The first part, "do justice," lines up with Jesus' blessing on those who "hunger and thirst for righteousness" (Matt. 5:6). Here, *righteousness* is the same word that gets translated elsewhere as *justice*. The beatitude says, in effect, "Blessed are those who so much want to see rightness happen, justice happen, that they hunger and thirst for it, they sacrifice, even suffer for it."

In a similar vein, Francis, addressing our basic structures of injustice, has caused no small stir with statements such as this from his 2013 document called *Evangelii Gaudium*:

> We also have to say "thou shalt not" to an economy of exclusion and inequality. Such an economy kills. How can it be that it is not a news item when an elderly homeless person dies of exposure, but it is news when the stock market loses two points?

Or this from his June 2013 address to the Food and Agriculture Organization:

> A way has to be found to enable everyone to benefit from the fruits of the earth . . . to satisfy the demands of justice, fairness and respect for every human being.

I think the reason that Francis is being heard is that he issues the calls for justice not from a papal throne but from a position of powerlessness, saying about church leaders, for example, that they need to be

> close to the people, gentle, patient and merciful; animated by inner poverty . . . and also by outward simplicity and austerity of life, and not have the psychology of princes.

This last quote, from a June 2013 address he made to papal representatives, known as Apostolic Nuncios, sounds a lot like Micah's instruction to "love kindness, and walk humbly with your God" and like these beatitudes of Jesus:

> "Blessed are the poor in spirit, for theirs is the kingdom of heaven.
> Blessed are the meek, for they will inherit the earth.
> Blessed are the merciful, for they will receive mercy."
> (Matt. 5:3, 5, 7)

Catholics and Protestants together, who are shaped by the gospel values of the kingdom, are reminded in Francis that they have so much more in common than whatever differences might have been important years ago.

Mission through Relationship

One of the most difficult things to explain before or after a mission trip is that we don't go to Guatemala to build things. We go to build relationships and to build understanding. We go to be present with people who have become our partners, just as we have become theirs. We go to know and to be known. That takes time. A relationship of trust and understanding can't be created in a single trip that lasts a week or even less. So we go back again and again. (I recommend Robert D. Lupton's *Toxic Charity* for more on this approach to mission work.) It can be difficult to grasp the notion that our presence, our being there, is a greater gift than anything else we might do there. We were told repeatedly, "We are so thankful that you have come to hear our stories, to know about us." It's only by being there and hearing that said, time and again, that it begins to sink in. One elderly lady in Herlinda's group said, "You have left your homes and your families and come from so far away to be with us."

We visited Eben-Ezer Presbyterian Church, a very small church in a remote location. The men are elsewhere looking for work, so the church is composed mostly of women and children. When Pastor Pedro was saying his thanksgivings for our coming to be with them, he got choked up recalling the name of a high schooler who had visited from our presbytery more than fifteen years before. I think that was his way of saying, "You have been coming for a long time. You have not forgotten us."

One pastor from another church had started riding buses at four o'clock in the morning—for four and a half hours—to have his two minutes to say thanks to us. Many others had come long distances as well to thank us for coming to hear their stories. Samuel said, "We thank you for coming to be witnesses to the importance of this program in our lives." Most of them said that they tell their congregations regularly about our presbytery and our partnership with them. We are there with them in their gatherings, even when we are not physically in their country.

One difference between Catholic and Protestant traditions, not just in Guatemala but around the world, is the opportunity for women to be ordained leaders in congregations. One Guatemalan female pastor said to us, "As a woman I am especially grateful for the opportunity to study, because for women such opportunities are limited. I have long had a desire to preach, and now I am more prepared to do so. I still remember a sermon that I heard years ago preached by a woman at a retreat. I said to myself that I would like to do that, too. Now I am closer. I talk through my studies with my eleven-year-old son, and sometimes he helps me make corrections to my homework. He says he wants to be a pastor too."

Making financial contributions makes a big difference for churches in poor countries, but it is the spirit of partnership that embodies Christ. As one leader said to us, "We have seen money given in other ways. You allow us to make our own decisions. You treat us as brothers and sisters going along the way together."

Relationships have power that even money and physical assistance don't. In November 2013, Pope Francis encountered a man in St. Peter's Square suffering from a painful, disfiguring genetic disorder. The man's head was covered in bulbous tumors ranging in size from peas to golf balls. That man has surely experienced rejection and isolation due to his condition, but Francis put his hands on the man's face, kissed him, and embraced his tumor-ridden body. The man knew that the pope had no medical expertise to cure him, and perhaps he did not expect a miraculous healing, but being touched and embraced—connecting in even a brief but real relationship—was a balm to the man's soul, and he wept.

When we build relationships, when we begin to know the other, only then do we discover our most basic and common desires to do justice and love mercy. And out of those common concerns can come communal action. The Catholic and Protestant women in Guatemala continue the quiet and profound work of addressing the health needs of their community. Unlike the cathedral and church in Guatemala City that sit opposite one another, these women come alongside one another to listen, to share, and to build something that does justice. Our common mission is about relationship. It's about helping women find their voice. It's about giving people the freedom to determine their own futures. It's about learning from our own mistakes and not continuing to do things that divide and cause resentment. Whether North American, Central American, Protestant, or Catholic, it's about being there and being with. That's how partnership works, even across the biggest divisions. That's all God's people doing justice, loving kindness, and walking humbly together.

Let's Talk about It

1. The Protestant writer of this session says he had "more in common theologically with the priest in town than . . . with most of the Protestant pastors" in the small towns where he used to live. Do you

know people from other traditions well enough to know whether you share much theological common ground? Have you been to their worship services? If so, what were your impressions? What questions do you still have?

2. The justice, kindness, and humility God is said to require in Micah 6:8 is presented as the alternative to offerings such as livestock, oil, and even one's firstborn child. What are the things today that we are often tempted to offer God and others instead of the things God truly desires from us?

3. What would it look like if you and your congregation did justice, loved mercy, and walked humbly with God alongside people from a different faith tradition? Would this experience be focused primarily on action or fellowship? Might there be opportunities when you are together to learn about what's important to members of the other tradition?

4. Do you think that because Francis "issues the calls for justice not from a papal throne but from a position of powerlessness" this makes a difference in the way he's received, especially in an American culture that seems not to value powerlessness? Is it possible to "walk humbly" while living in luxury and holding a powerful position?

5. If "being there" is so important, what is the value of sharing our own stories and learning the stories of other people? If you could tell people of other faith traditions your stories, what would they be, and what difference might it make that others hear them? What opportunities have you and your congregation created to hear the faith stories of others?

Chapter Four

Set Free

Then Jesus said to the Jews who had believed in him, "If you continue in my word, you are truly my disciples; and you will know the truth, and the truth will make you free." They answered him, "We are descendants of Abraham and have never been slaves to anyone. What do you mean by saying, 'You will be made free'?"

Jesus answered them, "Very truly, I tell you, everyone who commits sin is a slave to sin. The slave does not have a permanent place in the household; the son has a place there forever. So if the Son makes you free, you will be free indeed.

John 8:31–36

There is a story of two young American soldiers who became dear friends as they fought side by side during World War II. After one was killed in battle, the other risked his life to bring his friend's body to a small French Catholic church, where a priest assured him there would be a proper burial. The priest also asked if the deceased

.. as a Roman Catholic. His friend didn't think so but affirmed that he was a great man and soldier.

Years later, the surviving soldier made his way back to that rural area of France to pay tribute to his friend. After the war, he had connected with his friend's family and had learned that his friend, indeed, had not been raised Catholic. He also learned that the church would not have been allowed to bury his friend within the official church cemetery, due to the belief that the yard within the fenced grounds represented the kingdom of God and that only members of the true church—that is, the Catholic Church—could be buried there.

Upon traveling to France and reaching the small church, the soldier searched among the graves beyond the churchyard but couldn't find his friend's gravestone. Frustrated, he eventually made his way into the old church, where he was surprised to find the same priest who had helped him years earlier. When the man inquired about his friend's grave, the priest took him to a plot with a simple headstone just inside the fenced yard. Confused, the man spoke up, "But he wasn't Catholic. I've read your rule books. He should have been buried outside the fence." The priest looked up at him and with a twinkle in his eye said that he, too, had searched the rule books and didn't see anything that would prohibit him from moving the fence.

That's what this book is all about. We are not seeking to deny or do away with differences in theology or doctrine or church history. We just want to make sure that, in the midst of all the guidelines and fence lines and rules, we are still making the church as expansive as God's love seems to be. Sometimes that requires moving a fence or two, because often the things that keep us feeling left out or locked up are shackles in life that can, in fact, be adjusted or unlocked—or perhaps already have been.

Free Indeed

One of the most overwhelming and terrifying realities we are confronted with in life is not that we are slaves but that we are free. Forgiven. Liberated. Free to live and try and fail and forgive and love and feel unloved. We are free to join fully in the mission of God's expansive love. Yet as much as we say we yearn for freedom, the fact is that fences feel much safer.

In John 8:32, Jesus tells his followers, "You will know the truth, and the truth will make you free." They were confused by this, reminding Jesus that since they'd never been slaves, there was no need to be set free. Jesus replied, "Very truly, I tell you, everyone who commits sin is a slave to sin. The slave does not have a permanent place in the household; the son has a place there forever. So if the Son makes you free, you will be free indeed."

In exploring this passage and its implications, I believe that we can discern three types of fences or shackles that keep us from living in the freedom that is ours in Christ—fences or shackles that also often hinder us from participating in God's mission in the world.

The first fence is perhaps best described as a fence of omission: in other words, our denial that there is any problem at all. This is clearly on display in our reading. Jesus is talking not to the masses but to those who had believed in him, those who were following him. He says that if you continue in my word, you will be free. And how do those who believed in him respond? They channel Robert DeNiro in *Taxi Driver* with their indignation: "You talkin' to me? Are you talkin' to me? *We're* descendants of Abraham; we've never been slaves to no one! What do you mean, 'You will be made free'?"

Never been slaves? What? The scope of their denial is blinding. Historically, factually, they were dead wrong. Somehow they'd forgotten Egypt, Assyria, Babylon—all places Israel had literally been enslaved. And then, apart from this physical bondage, there is a tendency woven into our human constitution that leans toward disobedience. As the Apostle Paul put it bluntly, we are slaves to sin. We are inherently broken. So the first fence is this: We do silly, hurtful, broken things, not because we're just having an off day, but because we're sinners. And Jesus points this out not to chastise us but to free us. When you've struggled with the painful or confusing symptoms of an illness for many years, it may be hard but it's actually a relief to hear a clear diagnosis. Only then can proper treatment and lasting recovery begin.

A few months after Francis's election, Antonio Spadaro was allowed to interview the new pope, and many of Francis's comments blew up in worldwide media. Spadaro's first question was this: "Who is Jorge Mario Bergoglio?" After considering his response for some time, the pope's answer was this: "I am a sinner. This is the most accurate definition. This is not a figure of speech. I am a sinner."

But then you look at this pope and wonder: How can someone whose primary definition of himself is "sinner" seem to be so happy and peaceful most of the time? The answer is in his profession. I would contend that it's precisely because he knows he is a slave to sin. He knows that he can't do it on his own, that he needs help. That's the freedom and joy that self-honesty brings. The pope was telling the truth. The truth sets you free, and true freedom feels good.

That is the first set of shackles we must unlock on our quest for freedom. But once we take that first step out of the closet of denial or self-righteous deception, two more shackles are ready and waiting to trip us up in our liberation journey. They follow this first step toward freedom in two opposing but equally unhelpful ways.

The first response to the truth of brokenness is one of defeat: *I am a sinner, and there is no hope. Because of my sins, because of my faults and failures, I allow myself to be locked in guilt and condemnation. I am crushed, weighed down by the chains of worthlessness.* Although we can empathize with the burden of this reality, it is, my friends, a lie.

The other response to the reality of our human condition is to steel ourselves against it and to apply a Puritan work ethic. This shackle says that *if I discipline myself—* or, for some of us—*if I punish myself long enough, if I deny myself and if I work hard enough, or if I pray long enough, penalize myself thoroughly enough, go to church often enough, serve enough, act nice enough, then somehow I will be able to claw my way back into righteousness. I will be able to please the God who has authority over my desperate state.* While it may feel as if we can make progress through self-castigation or discipline, we cannot, by this means, achieve the freedom and absolution our hearts desire. Yet another shackle.

I read an August 1, 2005, article in *Christianity Today* from our Protestant pope, U2's front man, Bono: "Although the idea of Karma and an eye for an eye, reap what you sow, seems woven into the fabric of life and relationships, grace interrupts this natural law. Jesus' life, death and resurrection interrupt the economy of reciprocity and we are forgiven." Amen. Preach it, Bono. We are forgiven, truly and completely. The one whom the Son sets free is free indeed! Free from blame, free from punishment, free from the past, free to be thankful, free to love, free to hurt, free to join in the mission of advancing God's will in the world!

Here's the honest truth that absolutely blows our weary hearts and minds: God never grows tired of forgiving. Never. I do, you do, even Pope Francis does. We all grow tired of forgiving and of asking for forgiveness. But God's capacity for granting absolution and freedom is apparently limitless. We are free, today and tomorrow, no matter what. Period. And we are freed not just to know the love of God in the depths of our wounded souls but also to share that freedom, to be part of the mission of liberation and forgiveness.

This is something Francis and his order, the Jesuits, are all about. Jesuits voluntarily make vows of simplicity along with a commitment to a missionary life-style—to go where God leads them to share the good news of freedom and forgiveness.

Accepting Our Freedom

One of my favorite movies is another DeNiro film, *The Mission*. It is centered on the work of Jesuit priests in eighteenth-century South America. DeNiro plays a former soldier named Rodrigo who would ride into the highlands, capture some natives, and then sell them into slavery. In a dispute over a lover, Rodrigo ends up killing his own brother, which causes him to seek refuge and punishment for his sins at the Jesuit monastery in the city. Disgusted with his life and what he has become, Rodrigo simply wants a cell where he can be left to die for his sins. The Jesuits are there as missionaries, called to carry Christ's love to the highlands, so the lead priest works out a deal with Rodrigo. Because he won't accept forgiveness from God through the words of the priests, Rodrigo will do penance. As penance, he will join the group of Jesuits as they make the arduous climb up a waterfall to live with and share the good news of Christ's love with the natives he had once enslaved. Rodrigo agrees, but only if he is allowed to drag his weapons and armor behind him in a massive net, in order to make the journey even more dangerous and difficult for himself.

After a long and grueling trek, the priests arrive in a jungle village, with Rodrigo slowly bringing up the rear, exhausted and knowing that he will most likely be killed by the natives once they recognize him. Indeed, this looks to be the case as a villager runs to the muddy and depleted slave trader, grabs a fistful of his hair, and forcefully puts a knife to his neck. Taking notice, the chief calls out to the villager, who then removes the knife from DeNiro's neck and methodically begins to cut the ropes binding Rodrigo to his weapons and armor. The tangle of metal is shoved from a cliff into the river. Disbelieving and free, Rodrigo breaks down sobbing. Villagers and Jesuit brothers surround him with hugs, tears, and laughter and lead him into a new life. Rodrigo the sinner is free.

Accepting that we have been set free can sometimes be harder than it sounds. For help practicing such acceptance, I'd like to suggest an Ignatian (that is, Jesuit) practice called the *examen*. It begins with taking a few deep breaths to calm yourself and is followed by inviting God simply to be with you. From that peaceful place, allow your mind to scan the recent past, take an inventory of the week, and answer these simple questions:

1. Where did I serve Jesus? Where did I miss serving Jesus?
2. What made me feel most alive? What drained me of life?
3. When did I have the greatest sense of belonging? When did I feel most fenced in and alone?

4. Where and how did I impart freedom? Where and how did I receive freedom?
5. When did I feel fully myself? When was I a self I did not want to be?

God longs for us to recognize, remember, and expand those things that have given us life—those things that have made us feel like we were walking in the freedom God has granted us. Continue to remember and name such things. Hold on to them, repeat them, and cling to them.

Name those things that have made you feel most fragmented, most drained, most locked up, and enslaved: sins, words, heavy judgments that swirl around your soul. Name the burdens, the bitterness, the regret, the expectations, the hurt, the failures that continue to lock you down and keep you from being free. Imagine those things engraved on heavy iron shackles. Feel their weight in your hands.

Now imagine Jesus beside you, putting his hands over yours and saying, "You needn't carry these any longer." Imagine standing on a mountainside with Jesus and together pushing those chains down into the chasm, so far down you never hear them hit bottom.

Hear and believe the words of Christ: Those whom the Son has set free are forever and always free indeed! We will always be sinners, but we are free from the burden of sin and its shame. We are free from condemnation, free from self-justification, free to join joyfully, fully, humbly in the mission of God.

Let's Talk about It

1. What would it look like to "move the fence" to enable a better relationship between Catholics and Protestants? Should, for instance, Protestants in

some way or other be subject to papal oversight? Or should Catholics open up the Eucharist fully to non-Catholics?

2. In what ways are "fences" more comfortable than the freedom God wishes for all of us? How does a preference for fences hinder ecumenical and interfaith relations? In what ways might shackles or chains of slavery be more comfortable for us than accepting the freedom God offers?

3. Recall Pope Francis's interview response, "I am a sinner. This is the most accurate definition. This is not a figure of speech. I am a sinner." What do you like about that answer, and what about it makes you uncomfortable? Would you ever use that as a description of yourself? Why or why not?

4. Jesus said, "If you continue in my word, you are truly my disciples; and you will know the truth, and the truth will make you free." In Christianity, the truth may be identified in doctrines and creeds, but ultimately, truth is not a doctrine but a person. How does knowing Jesus as the truth make you free? And if the disciples of Jesus are free, do they lose some of that freedom by dividing into such camps as Protestant, Catholic, or Orthodox?

5. What has enslaved you, either now or in the past? What have you done or can you do to free yourself?

Chapter Five

#selfie

Let the same mind be in you that was in Christ Jesus,
who, though he was in the form of God,
did not regard equality with God
as something to be exploited,
but emptied himself,
taking the form of a slave,
being born in human likeness.
And being found in human form,
he humbled himself
and became obedient to the point of death—
even death on a cross.
Therefore God also highly exalted him
and gave him the name
that is above every name,
so that at the name of Jesus
every knee should bend,
in heaven and on earth and under the earth,
and every tongue should confess
that Jesus Christ is Lord,
to the glory of God the Father.

Phil. 2:5–11

World leaders, from kings and queens to presidents and prime ministers, are typically surrounded by teams of advisers whose job it is not just to keep their leaders informed about things they must know but to keep their leaders from looking foolish. Rule #1: Don't let your leader be photographed in ridiculous headgear.

Pope Francis has given his inner circle a run for their money since his election. His security staff is in constant anxiety over their leader's tendency to abandon protocol in order to get closer to the people—and however inadvisable image consultants might find it, he is never afraid to look a little silly.

One image that made the rounds on morning shows and social media featured the pope sporting a clown nose with a newlywed couple. The couple had just married at the Vatican and was part of a charity that uses clowning to cheer up ill children in hospitals. Francis came to congratulate them on their marriage and to show appreciation for the work the charity does by donning part of their "uniform."

In Brazil, Francis watched a performance of native dancers. One of the dancers took off his headdress to give to Francis as a gift. But the pope did more than just accept the headdress; he put it on and wore it for a while.

When he visited a mine in one of the poorest regions of Italy, Francis dutifully wore a bright yellow hard hat, complete with headlamp, with his long, white robes.

This pope never lets concern about his appearance or what people will say get in the way of connecting with people—even little children, who as we all know, can be quite unpredictable. When Francis interacted with a certain little girl, he took off his skullcap to let her try it on. While giving an address at the Vatican, a little boy escaped the crowds and showed up on the platform next to the pontiff. Security guards found some candy and offered it to the boy to convince him to come down off the stage. But the boy wouldn't leave, and Francis didn't seem to mind.

One of my favorite of Francis's less distinguished moments on camera is a photo taken while the pope was interacting with some teens in St. Peter's Basilica. Francis was squeezed close together with two teen boys and one girl, the girl's dark-polished fingers gripping a blue smartphone as she took a selfie with the pope. *Selfie*, Oxford Dictionaries' 2013 word of the year, might not even have been in the pope's vocabulary, but connecting with people of all ages certainly was.

Time magazine named Francis its 2013 person of the year, nicknaming him "The People's Pope." And that's who I see when I look at these pictures. Pope Francis is an incredibly winsome figure to me. He seems to be the kind of guy who I would want to be friends with.

Francis is the people's pope without diminishing any of his popeness. Instead, he is redefining what it means to be pope. He doesn't give up any of his papal authority; he doesn't shirk any of his duties. He holds the two in a beautiful tension—his call to serve with and for the people, and also his understanding of the inherent otherness of the authority of his position. The more we think about Francis and the things he stands for and the reasons people are talking about him, the more I begin to realize that the part of me that is drawn to Pope Francis is the part of me that is drawn to Jesus.

God in Human Likeness

Jesus is the people's Christ—the Messiah who, Paul writes, "did not regard equality with God as something to be exploited, but emptied himself, taking the form of a slave, being born in human likeness" (Phil. 2:6–7). You can almost imagine God's inner circle, the top angels of the heavenly host, saying, "But Lord, that will look *ridiculous.* People will laugh at you. Why would you set aside your glory like that?" I can hear God saying in reply, "Let them laugh. Let them know I'll do *anything* to connect with them." Jesus came to us, fully human and yet fully God, a Messiah who doesn't give up any of his divine authority, who doesn't shirk any of his duties. Jesus embodies this beautiful tension that we're so impressed with in Pope Francis.

This understanding of Jesus is implicit in so many stories in the gospel. Jesus of Nazareth offers an invitation, and at once people leave their jobs and follow him. Jesus has to climb up a mountain to give a sermon because there are so many people who want to listen. Jesus is so full of grace and love that after his death a member of the opposing political party begs to be allowed to care for the body.

This is the kind of love that tugs at our hearts, that begs our allegiance. This kind of winsome love draws the attention of Catholics and Protestants across the world. It's the kind of love that causes fishermen to drop their nets and follow an unknown rabbi.

Francis is the people's pope. He is a loving pope, but not just loving in a way that is painful and sacrificial. Rather, he seems to delight in sharing life with all kinds of people. I would imagine that if Pope Francis were given a choice, a selfie might not be his preferred method of photography. I would guess that he has probably had much more experience in his almost eighty years with his picture being taken in a more traditional way, but in looking at the picture of the pope with the teens, you sure can't tell. He's willing to engage with the people around him on their terms, and he doesn't seem to hate it. He seems to delight in connecting with these teens in a way that is significant to them.

I think that one picture speaks volumes about how Francis loves. I wonder sometimes about the way we talk about love in the church. Ask any Sunday school kids how they know that Jesus loves them, and the answer you'll get nine times out of ten is "because he died on the cross for me." And it's completely true. God demonstrates his love for us in that while we were still sinners, Christ died for us. But the beauty of what Francis reminds me is that not only does God die for me but God delights in me.

I spend a lot of time with kids, and I love the kids and youth of my church. As any parent knows, sometimes loving kids demands toughness, sacrifice: *No, you can't climb onto the roof no matter how fun you think that sounds.* Or *Let's sit down and have a conversation about the choices that you're making right now.* But often it is a delightful sort of love: *Of course I want to grab breakfast with you. I'd love to come watch your basketball game. Tell me more about what your friends are up to. I love you, and I want to be around you.*

The selfie of Pope Francis reminds me of the love that is both sacrificial and delightful. It reminds me that there is a God willing to take the form of the slave, willing to be found in human likeness, to be obedient unto death. As the author of Hebrews says, "We do not have a high priest who is unable to sympathize with our weaknesses, but we have one who in every respect has been tested as we are, yet without sin" (Heb. 4:15). We have a God who knows what it's like to be human and yet delights in saying, "Approach the throne of grace with boldness." That is a beautiful love.

Share the Delight

We never receive the love of God only to keep it for ourselves. As our understanding of the way God loves us increases, so too should our understanding of the way we have been called to love the world. We are always blessed in order to be a blessing, so I just wonder this: How well are we doing at loving people? How well are you doing at delighting in people? How well am I doing at enjoying the company of others—those who are like me and unlike me?

A picture popped up on my Facebook wall recently. It was a selfie that my church's Outreach and Hospitality Committee took after a meeting. A goofy group of smiling faces—at a committee meeting! That's not like most committee meetings I'm aware of. Amid important issues and plans to be discussed, the committee members are delighting in each other.

What a beautiful picture of the people of God loving each other. I look at that picture and am reminded of what a privilege it is to be allowed to love the world. God didn't go to such great lengths to be near us in order to condemn us or shame us, but to love us. God showed us how wonderful it could be to set decorum aside and just delight in people.

So, in honor of Francis and his extravagant love, in honor of the way that he reminds us of an extravagantly loving God, let's make for ourselves a digital reminder of God's delight in us and the delight we can experience in one another. If you have a smartphone near you as you read this book or discuss it with a group, grab it now and take a quick selfie. If you have other people around, squeeze in and capture the moment together. Make a funny face. Delight in God's love and the joy of loving and being loved.

The One who was born in human likeness loves not only with great sacrifice but with great joy. How delightful it is to love and be loved in the way that we love and are loved by God, a high priest fully able to sympathize with our weaknesses. This God is the One who invites us to the throne of grace, who invites us to love others with unabashed delight.

Let's Talk about It

1. What do you think when you see a world leader (political or religious) doing something silly—wearing a costume or a funny hat, or just laughing and having fun? Does your reaction depend on your previous impression of that person, whether you already liked or agreed with him or her?

2. When you hear Jesus described as "the people's Christ," what does that mean to you? Does it mean that Jesus doesn't care about people who might be described as members of an elite class or as wildly wealthy? What do the Scriptures mentioned in this chapter (Phil. 2:5–11 and Heb. 4:15) mean for your faith?

3. In thinking about "the kind of love that causes fishermen to drop their nets and follow an unknown rabbi," describe what it was that caused you to be a disciple of Christ, if you are one. Do you think that this attraction to Jesus is somehow different for Protestants and Catholics? If so, how?

4. Do you agree that "as our understanding of the way God loves us increases, so too should our understanding of the way we have been called to love the world"? In what ways have you been called to love the world, to be a blessing to others? How has that grown or changed over time as you understand God's love differently? How might our efforts to show God's love be even more effective if Protestants and Catholics found ways to work together?

5. Whom do you see when you take a selfie? Whom do you think God sees? How big is the gap in those two perceptions—and why is there any gap at all? How might our difficulty in seeing how God delights in us affect our ability to delight in one another?

Chapter Six

Dumbing It Down

Now all the tax collectors and sinners were coming near to listen to him. And the Pharisees and the scribes were grumbling and saying, "This fellow welcomes sinners and eats with them."

So he told them this parable: "Which one of you, having a hundred sheep and losing one of them, does not leave the ninety-nine in the wilderness and go after the one that is lost until he finds it? When he has found it, he lays it on his shoulders and rejoices. And when he comes home, he calls together his friends and neighbors, saying to them, 'Rejoice with me, for I have found my sheep that was lost.' Just so, I tell you, there will be more joy in heaven over one sinner who repents than over ninety-nine righteous persons who need no repentance."

Luke 15:1–7

I remember the first time I approached the church where I would soon be called to pastor—a stone, gothic structure on a charming corner in Kansas City. I was impressed then, and I continue to be thankful for my affiliation with this classic, well-established, metropolitan church with a talented, astute, big-hearted congregation.

And it's a well-educated, professional congregation, I might add. Eleven percent of the American population holds a graduate degree, but here at Second Presbyterian, 75 percent of our current elders have masters or doctoral degrees. It's sort of cool knowing the former president of this corporation, or the CEO or CFO of that company, or the general counsel for that large organization, or a partner at that big law firm, or that renowned doctor, or that celebrated author, or that chair of such and such a board, or that brilliant engineer or artist sitting just a few pews in front of me. I like it that we go to the same coffee hour and that some of us study and pray in the same small group. Second Church members have been city leaders. There are some very successful, hardworking souls in this congregation.

As is the case with many congregations, our building, our worship style, and our giving—the "personality traits" of the congregation, if you will—reflect the demographics and values of its people. At Second, our personality reveals that we try to do things by certain standards. We take our theology, our responsibilities, and our work seriously. We study, we improve, and we demonstrate our commitment to excellence in mission, ministries, and events in ways that are intentional and thoughtful.

Maybe your church sounds similar, or maybe not, but either way, your church has certain characteristics that make it unique, and chances are you chose that church because it was different from other churches in some important ways.

Many of us who belong to mainline Protestant churches today do so because we have known or experienced churches in the past where a strict, literal interpretation of Scripture was enforced in ways that felt contorted in order to advance the agenda of the day. Many of us have been turned off by emotionally manipulative or guilt-based teachings or by organizations where one or two charismatic leaders set the tone and dictated the plan. Instead, we do our best to understand the cultural rootedness of our own limited perspective, and we welcome the views of other cultures and the writings of feminist, Catholic, evangelical, and Jewish scholars. Beyond that, we're involved in interfaith dialogue and in the stewardship of our earth and resources.

Those of us in "high church" traditions—which includes not only many mainline Protestants but most Catholics as well—have preferences for traditional music and theologically rich preaching, often because we disliked what we'd experienced in other churches as simplistic and shallow. We like the deeper waters of biblical and cultural contextualization. We also appreciate the various perspectives and insights we receive from intelligent and experienced people sitting next to us or through scholars such as Paul Tillich and Barbara Wheeler.

Many of us, both Protestant and Catholic, feel more worshipful singing hymns than praise choruses, more stimulated by intellectual sermons than emotional testimonies, and more comfortable in a pew-lined sanctuary than a dimly lit auditorium. I am definitely one of them. But the nagging question I can't seem to shake—and this new pope isn't helping—is what exactly intellect or comfort has to do with following Jesus. This Jesus didn't talk a lot of systematic theology, but he talked a whole lot about fishing and farming, about tending sheep and finding the lost.

Dumbing It Down

I've got this recurring gig that keeps my Sunday mornings pretty booked, but on occasion I get a chance to visit other worship services. Often I am encouraged, challenged, and thankful for what I find. But more times than I like to admit, I am made uneasy. Sometimes I walk into a sanctuary that feels a little more like a mall than it does a place of worship, and the band up front is repeating (over and over and over) a theology that I don't agree with, and the preacher begins to unpack a half-baked interpretation of Scripture without assuming or even caring that I have brought my own critical mind with its opinions and thoughts that morning.

Sometimes high-church Christians like me will categorize this form of church, this way of communicating the gospel, as "dumbing it down," as "shallow," as appealing to the "lowest common denominator." Many of us think such things, but we rarely say them aloud. That's because when we do, we hear ourselves. And the attitude of spiritual hubris is too sharp to miss. You may even have sensed it earlier in this chapter, when I explained why I prefer one style of worship over another.

In the last chapter, we explored Pope Francis's joy and his willingness to wear silly hats and pose for selfies with teens. For many, this shift has been welcome; for others, it has been unsettling. As *Time* magazine's article naming Pope Francis the person of the year for 2013 put it, "The giddy embrace of the secular press makes the pope suspect among traditionalists who fear he buys popularity at the price of a watered-down faith."

Simple, silly, accessible, watered down. And since he has not been so black and white and so doctrinally precise as his scholarly predecessor, Francis's tonal shifts have unsettled many, who feel he is moving too quickly away from conservatism and tradition and the respectable role of the supreme pontiff.

Some might say that Francis has dumbed things down, that he's made his office too ordinary, too commonplace. They might say that he is not precise, not respectable enough. Yet he continues to challenge church leaders to move out of the vestry and onto the streets—the dirty and simple streets. In his previous life, when he taught at a seminary in Argentina, Francis stressed how important it was for the students to feed and care for the sheep and pigs they kept on the grounds and to pray as they did so, because he taught that it is important to remember that God is found among the simplest of things and the lowliest of tasks. Francis also stressed the importance of going out to the barrios to practice teaching the catechism to children, because someone who could communicate biblical truths in a way that children could understand was truly wise.

Like the scribes and Pharisees we read about in Luke 15, Francis's critics seem to be "grumbling and saying, 'This fellow welcomes sinners and eats with them.'" Francis's response seems to be a lot like Jesus': "Which one of you, having a hundred sheep and losing one of them, does not leave the ninety-nine in the wilderness and go after the one that is lost until he finds it?" The children, the teens, the poor, those who just don't connect with the way "church" is being done: these are the sheep Francis—like Jesus—is willing to leave the ninety-nine to chase after.

It was impressive when Francis was on the cover of *Time* magazine as person of the year, but then he was on the cover of *Vanity Fair* in Italy. Then he completely backslid out of the sophisticated publications, and his face showed up on the cover of *Rolling Stone*—not the cover of the *National Catholic Reporter* or *Christian Century* or the *Periodical for Sacred Music*, but *Rolling Stone*.

Attendance at events in the Vatican has been overflowing. Tickets to Rome around holy days in the Christian calendar are booked three years out. People are not coming to hear Benedict's erudite speeches or to witness the beauty and pomp of the high Mass. They are coming to see a pope who appointed many new cardinals, most of whom are non-European and many of whom come from the poorest nations in the world, such as Haiti and Burkina Faso. Becoming a cardinal, Francis reminded these princes of the church in a letter he sent to them when he appointed them, "does not signify a promotion, an honor or a decoration: it is a service that demands a broader vision and a bigger heart." He continued: "This ability to love more universally with greater intensity can be acquired only by following the way of the Lord: The way of lowliness and of humility, taking the form of a servant."

Making the gospel simple enough for all to understand—maybe there's something to this dumbing down of this professional, classical, sophisticated faith of ours.

Reaching the Lost

Why did Jesus talk so much about sheep and farmers and fishing? Because he lived in an agrarian society in which the majority of people tilled soil or worked with livestock or caught and gutted fish. His primary audience, those he sought out and carried God's message to, were not the trained scribes but the shepherds, the laborers, the fishermen, the lepers, and the prostitutes: the lost sheep.

Jesus is our example, our hermeneutic, and sometimes the wisdom of God can sound and look so simple. It can even sound dumb to someone as professional as me. But sometimes our ascent to the divine comes through allowing our sophisticated selves to dumb it down a bit.

Roger Olson, professor of Christian theology and ethics at Baylor University, wrote an article recently stating that if Christ were to walk into our upper-middle-class churches today, the first discrepancy he would notice—and critique—about our practice of faith would not be a formal heresy like Arianism or Pelagianism but something more inherent and pervasive. Olson said that the heresy we struggle with was most clearly and prophetically illuminated by twentieth-century Reformed theologian Karl Barth in volume 2 of his monumental work *Church Dogmatics*:

> When the gospel is offered to [us] . . . an acute danger arises which is greater than the danger that [one] may not understand it and angrily reject it. The danger is that he may accept it peacefully and at once make himself its lord and possessor, thus rendering it innocuous, making that which chooses him something which he himself has chosen, which therefore comes to stand alongside all the other things that he can also choose, and therefore control. . . . Wherever the gospel is proclaimed . . . it is exposed at once to the danger of respectability.

The danger of respectability. It's hard to look respectable when you're searching for wandering sheep.

Olson says that if we could name this heresy, it would be "the domestication of the gospel and the church," or, to coin a word, *respectablism*. As a pastor of upper-middle-class churches for the past twenty years, I would have to agree.

There is a lot of bad theology out there. There are a lot of questionable and unhelpful pastors and Christians who are peddling a gospel that is half-baked and packaged in containers and conveyed by methodologies that are shallow and meant to titillate or intoxicate the heart, soul, and mind. We have a responsibility to profess good theology. But when it comes down to it, if we cannot talk about what Jesus means to us and do so in ways that engage and convey care and conviction to the typical, the young, the simple, those who do not own suits or listen to Bach or read *The New York Times*, then we may have lost our way. We, in fact, could be the lost ones Jesus is looking for.

My prayer for myself and for the church is that we would have the guts to descend, at least a few rungs, from our places of educational and ecclesial respectability, that we might grow more common and dirty and accessible in our pursuit of and care for the lambs that Christ is longing to gather into the flock, ourselves included.

For I tell you, there will be more joy in heaven over one sinner who repents than over ninety-nine righteous persons who need no repentance.

Let's Talk about It

1. Are the qualities attributed to Second Presbyterian Church and other well-educated, high-church congregations the most important when it comes to being the body of Christ for the world? If not, what qualities are? How would you describe your congregation? Does it have the qualities it must have to minister to the needs of people inside and outside the walls of the church building?

2. Have you experienced churches with different styles or different teachings? Do you agree that "there's a lot of bad theology out there"? If so, how do you experience that? How do you identify it? How does a Catholic or Protestant know that it's not just good theology offered from a different tradition? And when you encounter bad theology, what obligation do you have to challenge it?

3. Why do you think some people (maybe even you) find less traditional or more simplistic religious expressions unsettling? Do you think it is still true that "Francis's tonal shifts have unsettled many who feel he is moving too quickly away from conservatism and tradition and the respectable role of the supreme pontiff"? Who are the figures in Protestantism who seem to unsettle the religious establishment (however you define it)?

4. Pope Francis is quoted here as saying, "[The] ability to love more universally with greater intensity can be acquired only by following the way of the Lord: The way of lowliness and of humility, taking the form of a servant." In what ways are you following the way of lowliness and humility, taking the form of a servant? Is that approach part of the culture of your congregation? If not, what can you do to make it so?

5. What do you understand to be the "danger of respectability," as Karl Barth put it? Has your congregation succumbed to it? If not—or at least if not completely—how is your church acting in a countercultural way, and what can it learn from Pope Francis to intensify that?

Chapter Seven

Exploring Our Differences

Now before faith came, we were imprisoned
and guarded under the law until faith would be
revealed. Therefore the law was our disciplinarian until Christ came, so that we might be justi-
fied by faith. But now that faith has come, we are
no longer subject to a disciplinarian, for in Christ
Jesus you are all children of God through faith.
As many of you as were baptized into Christ
have clothed yourselves with Christ. There is no
longer Jew or Greek, there is no longer slave or
free, there is no longer male and female; for all of
you are one in Christ Jesus. And if you belong to
Christ, then you are Abraham's offspring, heirs
according to the promise.

Gal. 3:23–29

On March 4, 1829, one of the more outlandish
and scandalous events in American history took
place. It happened immediately after Andrew Jackson's
inauguration.

Tradition dictated that the president hold an open house at the White House, at which time anyone could come and meet the president. Jackson was a popular figure, especially among those who were not a part of the Washington establishment. According to some reports, tens of thousands of commoners wearing mud-caked boots and displaying unrefined manners descended on the White House, jamming through the doors. Food was dropped on the carpet, furniture was tipped over, and vases were broken.

Apparently, the president ended up escaping the throng by a back door. Some said the White House smelled of booze and cheese for weeks afterward. Others said it was an embarrassment. Historians now know that those who wrote of the account in such dramatic fashion were also members of the political party that had just received an electoral trouncing. They were opponents not just of Jackson but of the new breed of American leadership he represented.

Andrew Jackson was the seventh president but the first president who was not a Founding Father or son of a Founding Father. He was born in the backwoods of the Carolinas and became the first congressman to serve from Tennessee. There was record attendance as he took the oath on the steps of the Capitol, and those common people who rode from the frontier in trains and coaches to help celebrate Old Hickory's inauguration were absolutely thrilled to be invited to the after-party at the White House.

Historians have concluded that while there was a huge crowd and some furniture was broken and the carpet stained, no serious damage was done. And whichever White House staffer had the idea of bringing tables and buckets of punch and beer onto the front lawn was a genius. It was an open house that became a block party—and then a street party. A new sort of president was in town, and Washington would not be the same for some time.

This is what happens when the invite list is expanded. A growing, inclusive circle pushes us into confrontations with other cultures and with different perspectives and approaches. The growing process can be slow and painful. But the thing that keeps invite lists from growing and circles of inclusion from expanding is not the pressure encountered from without but the reticence, insecurities, and fears from within.

Widening the Circle

The Scripture passage above is scandalous and gregarious and outlandish. Paul is writing to the churches in Galatia (in modern-day Turkey), who are dealing with some serious disagreements between Jewish Christians who had grown up kosher, circumcised, and orthodox but had recently transitioned to this new expression of Judaism called "the Way," and those who were being invited in but hadn't grown up Jewish. How does a community navigate its history, law, traditions, and identity when outsiders are added to the invite list?

Paul tells the Galatians that those laws about food and circumcision do not apply to them:

> For in Christ Jesus you are all children of God through faith. As many of you as were baptized into Christ have clothed yourselves with Christ. There is no longer Jew or Greek, there is no longer slave or free, there is no longer male and female; for all of you are one in Christ Jesus. And if you belong

to Christ, then you are Abraham's offspring, heirs according to the promise.

Recently, Pauline scholars such as E. P. Sanders, James Dunn, and N. T. Wright have been highlighting the reality that Paul was born and raised Jewish and that the first Christians were not Gentiles who accepted Christ but Jews who understood Christ as the promised one who would usher in the messianic age of peace. And so Paul's letters, especially the earliest ones, were written to and read by Jewish Christians and some newly incorporated Gentile believers who were continuing the fulfillment of God's promise made to Abraham and the Hebrew people.

What promise are we talking about? God's promise to bless all the earth:

> Now the LORD said to Abram, "Go from your country and your kindred and your father's house to the land that I will show you. I will make of you a great nation, and I will bless you, and make your name great, so that you will be a blessing. I will bless those who bless you, and the one who curses you I will curse; and in you all the families of the earth shall be blessed." (Gen. 12:1–3)

Through the prophet Isaiah, God explains this further: "I will give you as a light to the nations, that my salvation may reach to the end of the earth" (Isa. 49:6).

In the New Testament, the circle just keeps getting bigger. In Acts 1:8, before ascending to the Father, Jesus says, "You will receive power when the Holy Spirit has come upon you; and you will be my witnesses in Jerusalem, in all Judea and Samaria, and to the ends of the earth."

In his epistle to the community in Galatia, Paul is addressing a growing family. The circle has gotten bigger. The invite list has grown, and those who grew up in one paradigm are crying foul. "What? Wait a minute! *I* had to get circumcised. *My dad* had to get circumcised. Are you're telling me *they* don't have to get circumcised? Seriously? And they can eat pork! Whoa! What has happened to my synagogue?"

The spirit of Christ through Paul was challenging Jewish Christians to allow, to empower, to invite Gentiles in as full-fledged members of the family. And women! And slaves! Ever since, the church has been working either to advance or, too often, to recall this radical invitation.

A Truly Inviting Church

A few hundred years after Paul's letter to the Galatians, the Christian religion, now distinct from its mother, Judaism, finally settled in a bit, and church order was established under Emperor Constantine. Heresies were weeded out, and the successor of the Apostle Peter, or the pope, became controller of the keys of doctrinal leadership—and the invite list. Things stabilized.

Then in 1054, the Eastern Orthodox separated from the Roman Catholics. Five hundred years after that—just when things were established and proper again—the defining boundaries of the circle began to crumble. People such as Luther and Calvin and Zwingli sent out a whole host of new invitations, not in Greek or Latin, but in German and French. Then things started getting really messy. People began reading their Bibles by themselves and confessing their sins directly to God. As the invite list expanded and as people who were studying Scripture began to question church doctrine, many were aghast.

Strange new members of the family were pouring in, and they were wearing boots and acting inappropriately. Food was getting smashed into the carpet, and the church began to smell of cheese and beer.

And so we began to draw new boundaries and establish proper rules once again—which, honestly, is necessary. Families need order and rules if we're going to get along. But some of the rules that our Catholic friends felt they needed to enforce were and are confusing and hurtful toward the newest members of the church. As a Protestant, I must say I disagree with some of the boundaries Pope Francis inherited and has maintained as the keeper of the keys and the invite list. I disagree because I stand outside the gates with those who have not received full invitations to the block party.

While the past two pontiffs have been loving and wise, they were also clear about the importance of doctrine and church law and what sin is and who is in. In fact, under Pope Benedict's leadership, the Roman Catholic Church reaffirmed its conviction that it is the one and true church:

> Therefore, there exists a single Church of Christ, which subsists in the Catholic Church, governed by the Successor of Peter. The Churches which . . . remain united . . . , by apostolic succession and a valid Eucharist, are true. . . . On the other hand, the ecclesial communities which have not preserved the valid Episcopate and the genuine substance of the Eucharistic mystery are not Churches in the proper sense.

In other words, millions of Christians around the world who are not baptized Catholics are not part of the church. If I could gain an audience, I would ask Francis to renounce this declaration and send a new invitation to all who seek to follow Christ.

Although I applaud the positive statements and gestures Francis has made toward women and their leadership role in the church, he seems to be clear that inviting over half of humanity to serve in the priesthood will not happen anytime soon. Such interpretations of Scripture and tradition are misguided. What the letter to the Galatians affirmed two thousand years ago, the church still has not realized.

While we're at it, we might as well talk about gay and lesbian inclusion. Francis shocked many when he answered a reporter's question about homosexuality on a flight back to Rome by saying, "If someone is gay and searches for the Lord and has good will . . . who am I to judge?" Those powerful words of hope and affirmation for many who had been shunned and ostracized by the church for centuries were shared, posted, and retweeted around the world.

Yet the church's official position continues to be that "deep-seated homosexual tendencies" are "objectively disordered." None of my gay friends who love Christ and serve the church appreciates being dismissively categorized under such a heading.

Don't get me wrong. I don't point out where I disagree with Francis because we Protestants have achieved the promise that God proclaimed from Abraham through Isaiah, Paul, and Christ. I point this out to make us all aware that none of us has. In fact, Protestant denominations are similarly fracturing over the inclusion and role of women and LGBT individuals. And the painful truth that Martin Luther King Jr. observed forty years ago still holds true: The most segregated hour in the United States is eleven o'clock on Sunday morning, probably more so in Protestant churches than in Catholic ones. So one thing that unites us as Christians is that we've all got a long way to go to live into the reality that in Christ "there is no longer Jew nor Greek, slave nor free, male nor female." As the spirit of the resurrected Christ has continued to transform our hearts, minds, and relationships, we have also come to realize that there is no brown or black or white or red, there is no Methodist or Mennonite or Baptist or Presbyterian. We are all one in Christ.

I believe that today the Spirit is once again blowing and stirring and calling out to the church. At a time when the U.S. president is black and when the pope, whose throne sits in the center of the Northern Hemisphere, comes from South America and when the greatest male athlete of the 1976 Olympics is now a woman named Caitlyn Jenner, we are hearing the voice of God call out to the world that no matter our prejudice or taste or inclination, *all* are invited—male and female, Jew and Gentile, slave and free, Left and Right, gay and straight, North and South, Protestant and Catholic, you and me. All are invited because all are one in Christ Jesus.

In your family, in your neighborhood, in your workplace, in your community, who has been left out? Whom do you need to extend an invitation to today?

At the Communion table, at the Lord's Supper, at the eucharistic meal, *all* are invited to come and serve and lead and learn and teach and rest and be forgiven and restored in Christ. May God continue to give us the strength and courage to live into God's ever-expanding, radical hospitality.

Let's Talk about It

1. The Scripture passage from the book of Galatians is described in this chapter as "scandalous and gregarious and outlandish." Do you agree? If yes, what makes it so? And what other passages of Scripture or confessional statements of your branch of the faith would you consider properly described (in a good way) by such words?

2. When have you felt like an insider, even an elitist, who got to set the agenda and control the power? In those times, how did you treat or think about those who at that same time felt like powerless outsiders? How might you do things differently today? When have you yourself felt like a powerless outsider? During such times, how did the powerful insiders treat you?

3. Paul says in Galatians 3:29 that everyone in Christ is "Abraham's offspring, heirs to the promise." In what ways would you say that God's promise to bless all the earth through Abraham has been fulfilled through the Abrahamic faiths of Judaism, Christianity, and Islam? What primary gifts has each religion brought to "all the earth"? What do you find most beautiful about each of these faith traditions?

4. If you are Protestant, list your disagreements with Pope Francis and the Catholic Church. If you are Catholic, what disagreements do you have with Protestant churches (and maybe Pope Francis as well)? Would these disagreements keep you from finding common ground with people from the other tradition? How would you describe that common ground?

5. Using terms that are as specific as you can make them, what does it mean to you to say that "we are all one in Christ"? Does it mean that denominational differences don't matter? Does it mean that we should have only one Christian church for all Christians in the world? Does it mean that somehow we give up our individual selves, our personalities, to be in community? What do you love best about the "all one in Christ" idea?

Next Steps

There are many practical and personal ways you can respond to the chapters and discussion questions in this book and, more broadly, to the call to be engaged in ecumenical and interreligious dialogue. Almost certainly, the group with whom you participated in this seven-week study can suggest ideas appropriate for your particular situation.

As you think about your response, remember that not all ideas are of equal value. Some, if implemented without careful thought and planning, could backfire and make things worse. So go ahead and dream together, but before you rush off to put any of your ideas into action, discuss them with people outside your study group and outside your religious tradition to get a sense of how they might be received. When it comes to ecumenical and interfaith dialogue, sincerity counts, but it's not enough. It must be coupled with wisdom and an appreciation for how ideas might be received. It's easy in religious contexts to be tone deaf and not even know it.

To get your thinking started, we've compiled a brief list of next steps you might consider taking that are in harmony with the spirit of this book and the questions it raises. Some of these ideas will need to be adapted to your local situation, but they represent a place to start.

- Visit a Catholic Mass if you're Protestant, and visit a Protestant worship service if you're Catholic. Go with someone who can explain what's happening while it's happening and what it means.
- Ask a well-versed Catholic (or Protestant, if you're Catholic) to speak to an adult education class at your church about why he or she has chosen that tradition and what it looks and feels like from the inside.
- Form a Catholic-Protestant discussion group to read Pope Francis's book *The Church of Mercy* together.
- Explore the Vatican's website, http://www.vatican.va.
- Explore the U.S. Conference of Catholic Bishops' website, http://www.usccb.org.
- Explore the official websites of major Protestant denominations, including the Presbyterian Church (U.S.A.), http://www.pcusa.org; the United Methodist Church, http://www.umc.org; the Southern Baptist Convention, http://www.sbc.net; and others.
- If you're Protestant, get a copy of *Lives of the Saints* by Richard P. McBrien (New York: HarperCollins, 2001) or *The Avenel Dictionary of Saints* by Donald Attwater (New York: Avenel Books, 1981), and see if you can develop a deeper appreciation for some of the people honored by the Catholic Church and by the tradition of naming saints.

- If you're Protestant, get the latest version of *Handbook for Today's Catholic* (Liguori, MO: Liguori Publications, 1994) and see what you can learn about the Catholic Church.
- If you're Catholic, visit websites of Protestant congregations to learn about their activities and (widely different) statements of belief. To get the flavor of the authors' Presbyterian congregation, visit the website of Second Presbyterian Church of Kansas City, Missouri, http://www.secondpres.org.
- Find out if your community has an interfaith organization that sponsors gatherings and learning opportunities. An example is the Greater Kansas City Interfaith Council (see http://www.kcinterfaith.org).
- Read a book on world religions, and discuss it with a group from your church. (See the suggested reading list at the end of this book.) This will expand your knowledge beyond the Abrahamic faiths of Judaism, Christianity, and Islam.
- Form a group to read and study Stephen Prothero's book *Religious Literacy: What Every American Needs to Know—and Doesn't* (New York: HarperCollins, 2007).

Suggested Further Reading

Understanding All Faiths Better

Eck, Diana L. *A New Religious America: How a "Christian Country" Has Become the World's Most Religiously Diverse Nation*. San Francisco: HarperSanFrancisco, 2002.

Hill, Brennan R. *World Religions and Contemporary Issues: How Evolving Views on Ecology, Peace, and Women Are Impacting Faith Today*. New London, CT: Twenty-Third Publications, 2013.

Hinnells, John R., ed. *The Penguin Handbook of the World's Living Religions*. Rev. ed. London: Penguin Books, 2010.

McDowell, Michael, and Nathan Robert Brown. *World Religions at Your Fingertips*. New York: Alpha Books, 2009.

McLaren, Brian. *Why Did Jesus, Moses, the Buddha, and Mohammed Cross the Road? Christian Identity in a Multi-Faith World*. New York: Jericho Books, 2012.

Neusner, Jacob, ed. *World Religions in America*, 4th ed. Louisville, KY: Westminster John Knox Press, 2009.

Partridge, Christopher, general ed. *Introduction to World Religions*. Minneapolis: Fortress Press, 2005.

Prothero, Stephen. *Religious Literacy: What Every American Needs to Know—and Doesn't*. San Francisco: HarperSanFrancisco, 2007.

Scotland, Nigel. *The Baker Pocket Guide to New Religions*. Grand Rapids: Baker Books, 2006.

Smith, Huston. *The Illustrated World's Religions: A Guide to Our Wisdom Traditions*. San Francisco: HarperSanFrancisco, 1994.

Wogaman, J. Philip. *What Christians Can Learn from Other Religions*. Louisville, KY: Westminster John Knox Press, 2014.

Understanding Catholicism Better

Allen, John L., Jr. *The Catholic Church: What Everyone Needs to Know*. New York: Oxford University Press, 2014.

Cole, Richard. *Catholic by Choice: Why I Embraced the Faith, Joined the Church and Embarked on the Adventure of a Lifetime*. Chicago: Loyola Press, 2014.

Flinn, Frank K. *Encyclopedia of Catholicism*. New York: Facts on File, 2007.

Handbook for Today's Catholic, foreword by Cardinal John O'Connor. Liguori, MO: Liguori Publications, 1994.

Understanding Protestantism Better

Guthrie, Shirley C., Jr. *Christian Doctrine*. Rev. ed. Louisville, KY: Westminster John Knox Press, 1994.

McCormack, Bruce L., and Thomas Joseph White. *Thomas Aquinas and Karl Barth: An Unofficial Catholic-Protestant Dialogue*. Grand Rapids: William B. Eerdmans Publishing Co., 2013.

Migliore, Daniel L. *Faith Seeking Understanding: An Introduction to Christian Theology*. 3rd ed. Grand Rapids: William B. Eerdmans Publishing Co., 2014.

Plunkett, Stephen W. *This We Believe: Eight Truths Presbyterians Affirm*. Louisville, KY: Geneva Press, 2002.

Understanding Judaism Better

Cukierkorn, Rabbi Jacques. *Accessible Judaism: A Concise Guide*. Oxford: European Association of Judaic Studies, 2004.

Dosick, Rabbi Wayne D. *Living Judaism: The Complete Guide to Jewish Belief, Tradition, and Practice*. New York: HarperOne, 2010.

Understanding Islam Better

Daniel, Ben. *The Search for Truth about Islam: A Christian Pastor Separates Fact from Fiction*. Louisville, KY: Westminster John Knox Press, 2013.

Hewer, C. T. R. *Understanding Islam: An Introduction*. Minneapolis: Fortress Press, 2006.

Patel, Eboo. *Acts of Faith: The Story of an American Muslim in the Struggle for the Soul of a Generation*. Boston: Beacon Press, 2010.

Volf, Miroslav. *Allah: A Christian Response*. New York: HarperOne, 2011.

CPSIA information can be obtained at www.ICGtesting.com
Printed in the USA
BVOW06s0824210116

433752BV00013B/50/P